BARREL CHILDREN

poems by

Rayon Lennon

MAIN STREET RAG PUBLISHING COMPANY
CHARLOTTE, NORTH CAROLINA

Acknowledgments:

> *African American Review*: "Seaview Gardens," "Gil
>   Town," "Children with William Syndrome Have No
>   Racial Biases"
> *Callaloo*: "The Exile Files Home to Jamaica," "Chapelton"
> *The Main Street Rag*: "Strippers," "Barrel Children,"
>   "Acropolis Diner"
> *Noctua Review*: "400 Years Later," "Gilbert"
> *Rattle*: "Sky Beer"
> *Stepway Magazine*: "Red Night"

Library of Congress Control Number: 2016933198

ISBN: 978-1-59948-563-8

Produced in the United States of America

Main Street Rag
PO Box 690100
Charlotte, NC 28227
www.MainStreetRag.com

Then I believe that it is still possible, the happiness
of truth, and the young poet who stands in the mirror
smiles with a nod. He looks beautiful from this distance.
And I hope I am what he saw, an enduring ruin.
  —Derek Walcott, Midsummer (23)

Either I'm nobody, or I'm a nation....
  —Derek Walcott, "The Schooner Flight"

This is my letter to the world....
  —Emily Dickinson , "This is My Letter to the World"

No. Not this pig.
  —Philip Levine, "Animals are Passing from
    Our Lives"

The term Barrel Children *refers to, in particular, Jamaican children whose parents—compelled by social and economic challenges—choose to leave their children behind in Jamaica to pursue economic opportunities in other countries (particularly the United States of America, Canada and England). These parents then send back barrels full of food and clothes and other items to their children.*

Contents

Jamaica: Between Paradise

The Exile Flies Home to Trout Hall, Jamaica 3
Chapelton, Jamaica 5
Gil Town, Jamaica 6
Barrel Children 7
Seaview Gardens, Jamaica 8
Gilbert 10
In Trench Town, Jamaica 16
Trout Hall All Age School, Jamaica 18
Big Bro 20
School Girl killed by Bus in Jamaica 22
Letter to Jamaica 23
The Sun-blocking Baptist Church 24
Heathergale 25
Tanisha 26
The Country Bus 27
The Brown River 28
Krazy Glue 29
The Magic of a Four Season Year 30
First Love 31
In Grand Mountain, Jamaica 32
The Deported 34
Mona of Seaview Gardens, Jamaica 36
May Pen 38
Sestina to Patricia 39
Baptism 41
Sundays, Trout Hall, Jamaica 42
Sky Beer 43

New Haven, Connecticut, USA: Between Dreams

400 Years Later 49
Staring at Thirty 51
How Do I look? 53

Man Overboard 55
Sad House 56
Ex-wife 57
Interracial Porn 59
Divorce 60
The Reformed Racist 61
As a Boy in the Insane Asylum in Hartford, CT 62
I Knew I loved You When You Told Me You Had Cancer . . . 63
Navina 64
Kyra 65
Frederick-Douglas Knowles 66
Meghan 68
Trisha 69
Catherine 70
Strippers 71
Stripper in Glasses 72
I No Longer Had a Speech Impediment 74
Newhallville, New Haven 75
Lynnette 76
The Heaven Beyond What We Know of Heaven 77
Club 78
Ode to Lake Whitney, a Reservoir 79
The Club Bouncer 80
Another Gun Speaks 81
Midnight Promises 82
From the New Haven Green 83
New Haven 84
On the Night Obama Won the Presidency 86
Children with Williams Syndrome Have No Racial Biases . . . 87
Ferry Street 88
West Haven, Connecticut 89
Creep 90
Dancing with Hurricane Sandy 91
After a Divorce 92
On Hearing Jerk Fish Jamaican Restaurant Closed Down . . . 93

Acropolis All Night Diner 94

Helen of New Haven 95

My Alcoholic Barber 96

He Regrets 97

Status 98

Second Day of New Job as an Inner-city
    Employment Specialist 100

Out in the New Century 101

Whalley Avenue, New Haven 102

2am, New Haven 103

Red Night 104

Jamaica: Between Paradise

THE EXILE FLIES HOME TO
TROUT HALL, JAMAICA

I fly down and get off a country
bus to stand on the bridge, under
which I was baptized at nine, trying
to interpret the sunny language of the river
of voices in the air above the
water-hugged rocks and heat-ripened
breasts of girls who look up, hurling
stony insults my way. So I cross,
follow a yellow butterfly into the sunny heart
of town, where the colorful
wooden shop fronts are littered with the idle voices
of half-naked men, leering at school girls in baby
blue uniforms, while their wives labor in the surrounding
Ugli fields of Mr. Sharke, the good Englishman,
who built and named this town of no trouts, Trout Hall,
who once a year deploys his planes
to spray his neighbors and green alligator-skinned
Uglies, hybrid child of the orange, grapefruit
and tangerine. Everybody knows his slogan: "The Affliction
is only skin deep, the beauty is in the eating." Over
the cardboard church even the pigeons sound gospel
and I am moved by brooks as brooding
as the Bible; traffic flows the wrong way
and the English missionaries' sun-blocking peach
Baptist church is still empty, except for the cows
chewing mouthfuls of shadowy grass and the cricket players crying,
    "Out"
as the wheezing, rust-colored cars line up to cross the pocked face
of the palm-sheltered bridge. A divine
wind blows out the sun as I slip into a crowded
bar and down Red Stripes until I forget

who I am and announce to God that I am
trying to write a fiction greater than God,
a poetry to define our world.

CHAPELTON, JAMAICA

The sun-remembered beggars
don't beg anymore. Noon, the fluting blind man
walks into his Bible with frail fingers. Relief
comes with the blue khaki river
of Friday high schoolers to feed and feed
on the restaurant heart
of town. In the market, the vendors mob
that one stray customer while outside the black bust
of the Maroon Cudjoe looks down on the white
Catholic Church graves which make
great seats for lunchers who laugh over the dead.
Beside the rainbow shop, a broken standpipe
gushes all day, where kids from the primary school
come to cool their fried feet as brown
palms wave from the court yard. In front
of the white police station
two shirtless men fight over
the job of emptying
a garbage bin. The powerless clock tower
cannot sing. One man flings the other
against a bank, and the defeated man—
plotting murder—watches peaceful
clouds, the cruel sun, a black butterfly
writhing in the wind.

GIL TOWN, JAMAICA

The sun drinks from the incurable
potholed scars of the bridge, the grassy
gully and slick soccer players, the dripping
standpipes beneath bird-pecked plums
of humpbacked trees, the pissy
perfumy corners of the All-Age School,
the mother's milk in the ants' nests, the sagging lines
of whipping clothes, the dancing aluminum
basin of water like a gig on an old woman's
wrapped head, the sprinkled
obeah potions, cow cakes,
the bullied boy's tears, the sweet
chemical-rich Jerry curls of Samuel's
mother shouting from the hill of her voice
for Samuel discovering April in
the doggy orange grove, the sweat-
soaked cricket-tennis ball sailing into
the clouds as the new missionary
church closes the day.

BARREL CHILDREN

The barrels are blond with tattoos
of addresses in permanent markers
on their skins. I examine my father's foreign
handwriting. Hieroglyphic, looping and drunken.
It reads, "From: ...Connecticut, U.S.A. To: ...Trout
Hall, Jamaica." Sis, Bro, Mum and I
and the delivery men spirit the barrels up
the thirteen steps to our verandah on this skyless
day. Other Barrel Children in colorful outfits
have sprung up around the yard like sudden flowers
as Mum begins to uncork the barrel, complaining
how Customs snapped off the locks. The inside
of the barrel smells like a pageant contestant, mother
takes each item out slowly, school
books, church shoes, a TV (our first), a walkman,
touching each item as intimately as though
she were touching dad. The giant bags of rice
and flour sit on the bottom like anchors. Mother
puts the top back on the barrel and Sis and Bro
slump a little as a boy in the crowd behind
the hibiscus hedge screams how his father
sent him a bigger TV and alligator-skinned
church shoes. My sister reminds him
that he has never seen his angel
of a father and my brother reminds him that he
hasn't received a barrel in years. And I,
I pray for the grace and guidance of the missing
sun while looking at the TV like a window
into my father's world.

SEAVIEW GARDENS, JAMAICA

They are not graves, these lines
of low brickhouses pressed up
against each other like lovers. At night,
gunmen run track meets on our complaining
zinc. Our house is the height of me. Somewhere,
the courthouse the color of our mother, the English
Queen. Skeletal branches finger the empty
bowl of sky. A surly black breeze picks up
discarded lotto tickets off spiky gravel in narrow
lanes between houses and dumps them in
the swamp and trench. Across us the black face
of a house lined with blood-coily vines,
huge pines hanging low with chains of moon-
white vines as white as the drug-white
ropes of chains pulled off the vain necks
of dead drug lords; another house bored
with as many bullets as stars.
Behind, a house painted a distant lawn-green
where a Rasta, praying in its shadow, cannot
see bags of helicoptered U.N. rice raining in the heart
of Ethiopia, on Haile's graves. From a row
in the distance Bounty Killer's
voice shoots up from a sound system, "Poor
people fed up…," then dies back down
as black trees in the commons lose their wings.
A yellow coat of birds lift up a hill and I think
how well I can see when I'm wearing my new
glasses. There are no signs, but the name given
this project in school is Seaview Gardens,
though from here you can't see
the full black page of the Caribbean
Sea, 'cause factories like Good-

year and their snaking trenches surround us. And,
not many flowers here neither, not on the former dump
on which we live, though our rain-bowed houses are colored
with the blowing, cracked heads of daises, hibiscus, sunflowers—
colorful as foreign wigs on coughing girls,
with cream-mated faces, dubbed
Lilly and Rosetta, planted themselves
by the bloody issue of the trench, deep
in midnight heels, waving, calling out,
to a staggering number of soldier-nicked,
alcohol-fueled men as the God
of England shovels down dust-
colored clouds from back mountains
to bury us, it seems,
and the moon is a window
in our dark coffin, we feel.

GILBERT

[Jamaica, 1988]

It was 1988 and none of us knew
what a hurricane was. "My God,"
Mother said as Gilbert roared up
over the orange hills. I was four and what
I saw through the louvers was an army
of clouds spreading over the commons.
"Get in the house," Mother's ballooning
eyes said, but Big Sis, Bro
and I were already tucked in the house
behind Mother who'd been reflecting out
on the verandah all evening, waiting
to meet Hurricane Gilbert, thinking
to talk it down. The huge Jamaican flag beat
up the road. The circle of mountains
shrank from green to gray. Everything
blended in the lightening wind: the palms,
the church of God zincs, the All Age
School's barbwire fence, the orange trees. Our two
bedroom concrete box house, built on concrete-stilted
legs, danced like the Dancehall Queen. I said,
"Mother." Our dancing house grew dark.
The house light had died out earlier
before we in Trout Hall knew
what was coming for us. "Mother," I said
again. And then Mother was in the house
pushing us to push against
the hurricane door. "The key, the key,
the key," everybody was saying. The key
was always hiding. I unburied the key
from beneath the wicker chair and handed it
to Mother who said, "Get the windows."

None of us knew we were in the eye.
But we were in the eye and shockingly
unprepared. "Father"
would have known what to do and what
was coming had he not been on farm
work in America picking apples. I shut
the louvers. The gully grew
into a brown monster and the wall
of tall vegetation waved madly over it.
The gully couldn't stop growing over the low
stone wall and I knew fear knowing that after
years of taunting the gully as a coward
for not being able to rise up enough
to reach our rented house that this was the day
it would come for us, for me. The living
room was a horror movie. All mother's
china kept flying at us and smashing
on the forest-tiled floor. Mother
shepherded us to the bathroom, the only
place in the house not on crutches
of stilts. We hailed our next door
neighbors for hope. The maniac whispers
of the wind lessened in the bathroom
but rain drummed like a drunk drummer
on the roof. Any minute our roof would go
flying off or the gully would
come for us. Mother braved out with Big
Bro, an old seven, and Big Sis,
an evil ten. They went to pack
clothes in a barrel that "Father"
had shipped a while back from America.
They came storming back

into the bathroom and screaming
through the window through the hurricane
to the Mightses, whose concrete box house sat
smugly on a hill. Mother was not tall.
To reach the window she hopped
up on the toilet seat to shout until she lost
her voice and hopped down and Sis
hopped up and screamed too
and Sis lost her voice and Big Bro
climbed up and lost his fake gravelly
voice and jumped down and I climbed up
and shouted through the dam of my stutter
but there were the Mights' big girls,
four of them, in their room, laughing
at me like we were a comedy show
because mother had many times
told them that I was God's Son, when
they swore that my father wasn't
my father. I asked God to still spare a place
for me in heaven and middle-fingered them
and pretended to have lost my voice
and Mother brought me down. None of us
had a voice anymore. Mother left and lugged
back a suitcase of our stuff. I could tell
from the fear tightening her face
that the gully was at the ankles
of the house. She announced hoarsely
that we would hike across
the road to the higher ground
of the All Age School. Somebody said
it was madness. It might have been
Sis, who had long hated mother

for losing our father to America. Sis also
hated Mother for dubbing me God's Son.
Sis only spoke to me to call me a bastard. I felt
the hurricane was God coming for me,
and fell in love with the plan to go
outside. Sis tagged me a dummy
for stepping on her toe while we paced in
the prison bathroom. Mother
gave up her plan to swim over to the All
Age School. The house wasn't going anywhere,
she said. That much was uncertain. We were low
on kerosene oil and sleep. We couldn't dream
in the dark on the sheeted floor of the bathroom
as the rain and the wind whipped the house.
I thought we were inside God; that that
was how it felt to be inside God, stormy. Mother
spied out a bedroom window and reported
the gully was at the knees of the house
but assured us heaven wouldn't allow it
to reach us. It was so dark we all seemed to fall
asleep. Gilbert rocked us like babes in a crib.
By sunlight Gilbert had deserted us
and we stumbled out into a new world.
From our high verandah we could see almost
to the sea at the other end of the island and we were
in the heart of the island. Trees covered
the ground like a defeated army. The palms along
the road in front of the school had died without a fight,
their roots flapping in the kind wind. The gully
was a baby again and I felt like a fish
flapping on the bridge. The zinc-less All
Age School looked like a bald man. "This

would be as good a time as any to tell
you all," Mother began. "Your father
isn't coming back for a long time." Nobody said
nothing. We children had all
known without knowing. We stared around
at the damage done and we
descended the long front steps, fifteen steps,
in all, to our long yard. It broke my mind
to see the ancient sour sap tree dead, broken
in two. The gully sluiced brownly on. It had left
its marks on the legs of the house. It had stolen
all of Mum's potted flowers from under the house
and all of "Dad's" crocus bags of beer bottles,
but not his motorbike which Mother
had sold a few weeks before Gilbert when "Dad"
must have dropped the news that he wasn't coming
back, that he needed to remarry to get his green
card in Connecticut. I hopped up
the low flood wall and watched the gully
weaken under the bridge where that summer
the bully Moby, who survived across
the gully, had repeatedly entered me
from behind a day after his mother had left
to be a nanny forever in England. Moby
was so old. He was nineteen. I wanted God
to wash him away but the wall of trees
across the gully had held. I sat on the flood
wall and saw that the coconut tree in the Mights'
backyard had lived. Two heavy coconuts had once
fallen on my head from that tree when I was three
and Moby knew that made me
foggy. Beyond the cemetery the Church

of God had lost its gore-red roof. The bridge had
more incurable potholes. The sun
fell, buttering everything, the sky baby blues.

IN TRENCH TOWN, JAMAICA

Here we are born with the wound
of a trench cut under our feet. The sun
is another of God's lost gold
coins floating over us
as poison washes down trench
from the rear of a Goodyear
tire factory. It kills the air,
the chemical smell, toxic, as smoke
rises from factories like prayers.
Dogs, guns and men bark
at England and her scores of Jamaican
sentry. The trench, you see, knifes
south slicing our lives into East and West.
Grandmum's East tin house leans
two steps from the trench, this vein,
carrying most of the city's blood, shit
and garbage. From Grandmum's house it runs
red past Willer's black tin house, whose
Daddy was once shot by a West
and dumped with rubbish into it,
then past Lily's fragrant sea-blue house, for whom,
from upstream I'd dumped in buckets of lilies
and listened on Grandmum's
tin roof as Lily giggled with childish love on
her two front steps. Creeps down past
the blazing white church
with its gold spire poking heaven, past
Minty's house, where I'd helped up Alfry,
her red-eyed gay son, from it once upon a time, past
the graveyard silence of goalless gravel basketball courts,
past glimpses of trampled-brown grass, where last summer
soldiers killed ten East and five West, past Killerman's

slaughter house, who once shot over me
and Willer last Feburary as our paper boats raced
downstream, past there and finally
runs under the empty shell
of the hurricane-sacked high school, where Willer
and I'd escaped the day Killerman killed
Willer's Daddy, and mailed him bloody through
the trench to the Caribbean Sea.

TROUT HALL ALL AGE SCHOOL, JAMAICA

Resembles a derailed train. Twin, long, one-story, yellow
concrete buildings side by side with a courtyard
like a referee between them, a courtyard with the heart
of a concrete map in the shape of Jamaica. Whenever it rains
the courtyard fills like a bowl and kids learn how to fight mother
nature to keep the water out of their classrooms by emptying
the courtyard with buckets as the rain drums like a church
drummer on the zinc roof. Kids crossing angry
unbridged rivers are freed early, the boys in sand-colored
khaki uniforms, the girls in sea-blue uniforms.
A lone cherry tree stands like a pretty guard in front
of the principal's office. The principal has a voice like a bell.
The front gate can never stay fixed. The giant, red water tank
sits at one end like a submarine as the curry smell of the canteen
fills the minds of students. Lunchtime approaches like the promise
of summer. Chalkboards with legs separate classrooms. Students love
to peek under the chalkboards to see into another grade.
Out front, the chicken coop is as noisy as the classrooms.
Teachers silence their students by feeding
them knowledge. Ms. Dee whips anyone who looks
at her. You can smell the outdoor wooden bathrooms
from a town over. A cloud-brushing tree out back is home
to a nation of lizards. In the middle of the playfield,
the red cricket pitch sticks out like an undying wound. The bigger
kids eat their lunches on the white graves in the cemetery
behind Mears Church of God. The biggest kids spirit away
oranges from Mr. Sam's doggy orange grove, pick
wormy guavas, while listening to pigs squeal like opera singers
in their foodless pen. Some kids gorge on plums
from the family of plum trees separating the school
        from the playfield,
throwing up in classes. Jamaica's six heroes are painted on the face

of the school as the almond tree sheds leaves like tears. A ubiquitous
old lady sits on a stool under the coconut tree, her bread
case full of snacks, waiting for the flood of students, the school's
zinc roof blinding, the giant Jamaican flag flapping
    over the trampled
colors of a garden, the sour apple tree ripe with birds.

BIG BRO

When we were young, I once saw you
charge a bully on a bluff overlooking
a shadowy gully. A skinny kid, you stormed
the big-eyed bully with punches until the dazed
kid wrestled you to the ground and sat on you,
pinning your arms to your chest with his right
hand while punching you in the ears with his left
fist. The old razor-made scars on his cheeks
puckered like a nightmare. We didn't have a father
to teach us how to be iron men. Yet there you
were toughening up by taking blow after blow
to your ear in the hellish Jamaican sun, winning
while losing, your arms folded in defiance until us
boys pulled him off, you fake-grinning, the sun covered
in nomad clouds. I was a boy of God. You were left
to fight the reality of undiagnosed dyslexia, fight
back tears as your 4th grade teacher Mrs. Dee
planted you in front of the class
and opened a book and told you "read" and whipped
you for every misread word, which was every
word. You read and said things that were not on the page
and you lost her, but the whole school would steal
a look, and I know that killed you. At night in our room
you spoke and I wrote love letters for you to your many
girlfriends and then later listened to you enter them next
to me while I pretended to dream. You were too handsome.
I sometimes wrote "hate" when you told me to write "love"
in your love letters to girls, because I often loved the same
girls you loved for different reasons. Dad used to send
bookbags for me to go to school while you were left to carry
your books in the rain in your hand to school,
because they all said you wouldn't end up anywhere good.

You are a man now, playing the same games our absent father
did, with two kids under one and one on the way
but nothing short of the return of heaven could have
impressed me more than the day years later,
after that fight after school, in front of the whole
school, when you stood shoulder to shoulder
with the bully and looked into the heart of his eyes
and we all watched him back down.

SCHOOL GIRL KILLED BY BUS IN JAMAICA

The wind resurrected her ribbons, blue, red
and white. She seemed to be sleeping
peacefully in the heart of the road, her sea
blue uniform reddening, her insides
out. The villainous rainbow-colored bus rested
at the side of the road, a rear wheel caked
with blood. The crowd murmured that the dead
girl had gotten on the bus but didn't
get on well enough, and as the now-beaten driver
drove off she was sucked into the wheel.
And that when the girl's mother had heard,
her screaming was so loud you couldn't
hear it like a dog whistle. As dark
dropped like sand on the sleeping
beauty, I turned to the wooden post office
wondering if I had been blessed
with mail from father who lived
in America. A woman said, "This little boy
shouldn't be seeing this." I said, "I'm fine." "Life's
preparing him to greet death," an old joker said.
Then an ambulance whirled in and spirited
her away, blood stains like crushed roses
on the cross of the intersection.

LETTER TO JAMAICA

It wasn't yesterday I saw you
on American news being lashed like a slave
by a hurricane. Grandma would say it was God
if she were up today and not buried in stone, inside you.
Too many years now since you've been free
from the hands of England
for your children to be looting after God.
I heard God touched down in the tin city of Kingston
in the harbor and made his way north through hell,
ripping off the tin tops of houses like cans, tearing guns
from the stony grips of fleeing criminals, stomping on Godless
tent churches with his thunderous feet, washing out the streets,
and trenches with the tears rolling from his cheeks,
moving on. I hope he had time to visit
Spanish Town and rid the city of the unburied crack
whores with his windy breath. I didn't hear about May
Pen, that city, where masked men roamed like pigs
at night. That deserved a visit. I hope He
had strength to advance into the country, Clarendon,
chewing up sticks from canefields that never produce
nothing but heartaches. Tired, I hope
he stopped to drink from Minho River
with Ted and Mikey's soul in it. Fed rushing across
brown fields of mixed-up black and white cows chewing dirt,
on into the safe of the All Age School
and scared the little ones to read and pray. I hope
He climbed up Bull Head Mountain, woke Grandma from her
shady grave, ripped her from your rootless heart,
Jamaica, and dove back with her in his whirly arms
into the light-blue dream of the Caribbean Sea
on his way back to heaven.

THE SUN-BLOCKING BAPTIST CHURCH

The missionaries fly down every summer
to the giant peach, sun-blocking church
they built in the heart of our playground.
They are white as our sneakers. They hand out
second-hand glasses too strong for our third
world eyes. They hand out symbolic bracelets:
a white bracelet, they say, means purity and angels.
Red is the blood of Christ. Black means sin,
hell and Satan. They baptize us in their indoor
church glass pool, ignoring the voice
of the river. They say winter is like living
warmly in a freezer and the American anthem
is the heart of a good person. They feed us the foods
we love and God's truth. We boys have crushes
on the missionary girls, but only speak
to them about heaven and hell. We play cricket
and football on the worn side of the churchyard.
When the cricket-tennis ball hits the church
we call it a four. When the ball is hit over
the church's blinding, zinc roof it's a six.
But we can only play freely when the missionaries
are gone. Only a handful of residents attend
their sun-blocking church when the demigods fly
back to a place like heaven.

HEATHERGALE

At 10, I felt like the world's strongest man,
because you told me you would marry me
when I was 18, if I followed you
to the river and carried your aluminum basin
of dirty clothes on my head. I did, and wasn't there
something special about the river that day?
The way it flowed in shadowy sunlight as your hair
streamed out in the green wind and a light rain
prickled from a clear sky as you sat on a rock rubbing
your whites together to pry the stains out, fanning bugs
from your juicy nineteen-year-old yellow legs, your crooked
smile like lovers leaning on one another, your skirt
folded between your legs, heaven peeking out.

TANISHA

At thirteen, you already looked ageless,
like you were made of steel, the slender beams
of your legs supporting the temple of your torso.
You believed your heart was a god, your head
the devil. I was twelve and you were my school
days. It was the year mother had evaporated
from my life and I couldn't get over your flagging
white and blue hair ribbons, your velvety black
skin, your sunny lower lip, your neat sea-blue
uniform, your promising smile, your Queen's
English, your house in a garden in Old Harbour.
Of course, I never told you I loved you before
I left Jamaica, because love was a flight to America.

THE COUNTRY BUS

The country bus is pregnant
with country people on its way
to market in the city. Asthmatic
as a school girl, it crawls up
a mountainous hill. The conductors hang off
doors like handkerchiefs in their back
pockets as crocus bags of oranges
and yams fly off the pile on the head
of the bus. The 100-year-old driver thanks
God it's day, because the country bus
only has one lit eye, as it leans this way
and that way like an overburdened donkey.
It's the color of rainbows on a teary day
and when it limps into market everyone
stands around to watch it give birth.

THE BROWN RIVER

[Jamaica, 1990]

Rain gonged on the tin roof as the gully grew
into a brown monster. I watched from my bedroom
window as Sis stood in the whipping rain on the low
stone wall peering into the insane growing water
as dad left for good to hunt for a better life for us
in America. Sis was on the brink of thirteen
which, to me at five, seemed as far away
as America. Dad yelled for her to come down, but Sis
dipped one foot into the Milo-like sludge, stirring
it as the coconut and breadfruit trees shook their great
heads across the gully. Dad hissed and puffed
and rubbed his desert-bald head. He couldn't miss
his Air Jamaica flight, so he got into his friend's car
and they sailed off while Mom sat in the rain
on the verandah anchored to her heartbreak,
watching Sis court death. As the car disappeared
like dark, Sis hopped off the wall and stomped
towards the house as though there was nothing
between her and hell now.

KRAZY GLUE

What was sadder,
Mum, you tearing up
while Krazy-gluing your dentures
back together on the sun-drowned verandah
after dad had punched you in the mouth
and motorbiked off to be with his other
woman in May Pen—or us kids looking
in the tall grass for remnants of your wedding
ring after you had tried to keep Dad
from going by grabbing his motorbike
and holding onto it while he revved and yelled
for you to let go?

THE MAGIC OF A FOUR SEASON YEAR

Father flew home from America
when I was nine. He was twice
the man he had been before
he left Jamaica. He spoke flowery
English and complained
about our oven sun. He talked
about the magic of a four
season year. Fall, I imagined,
was like every woman undressing, winter
was like living in a refrigerated
hell, spring was greener than a newborn's
cry, summer was like finding a lost gold
coin everywhere. He wanted to fly up everyone,
except Mum, who cursed and cried
to God until Father left two weeks after
he had come. Mother said he had to fly
back to his other wife. But before he left
Father left his old clothes for Bro and me
to war over, so we would grow up
to be devils like him.

FIRST LOVE

At ten I entered heaven
for the first time. Her name was Mona
and she was a rose in Seaview Gardens,
the nightmare inner city. Mona
was seventeen and lying on the living
room bed when I got up. Summer
sunlight through the louvers
crept over her light body. She had on
white panties and a white bra, her blonde
wig sat on the reddened concrete
floor like road kill. I hopped on her bed and she
opened her eyes and then closed
them back. I felt around inside
her and she slapped at my hand
like I was a bug. Mona
wasn't my aunt. Mona had been found
in the blue-tarped market of downtown
Kingston by Grandma when Mona was little.
Whenever I was hungry and frightened
Mona would let me suck sweet
hot milk from her sunny
breasts while gunshots rained
around us, and gunmen raced away
from each other on our tin-topped roof
as the innocent scattered for their colorful,
pressed together brick houses. So that morning while
she pretended to sleep I pulled down her
bra and began sucking her breasts
and while she smiled I entered
and never left the memory of her.

IN GRAND MOUNTAIN, JAMAICA

The earth is redder than the blood
of skinned hogs and sticks to your white
shoes and hands. I feel like a murderer
every time I cut a cabbage head out
the ground; rumor had it light was coming
here, but that's been thirty years now
and so we still use candles and kerosene
lamps to light our white nights. The dying sun
is something powerful when I'm standing in
it this high; I wear no shirt, just my khaki
pants from my school boy days. You should
see the way the sweat timbers down my scarred body
as somewhere in the green day the goats
bleat for water. From here one can almost
mistake that stony hill for a cemetery,
but no, here we bury the dead in
our backyards away from the wells.
When I was young I used to think
when I was finally allowed to climb
this high I would be able to see
clear to freedom of the Caribbean Sea,
to the impossibly tall hotels and careless tourists
but no. From here is just more cabbage hills
punctuated by lanky pear and star apple
and coffee and breadfruit trees, all growing
in the furnace of the sun. Me too. Thirsty,
I head to the two story concrete shop down in the valley
that burnt up a while back with my mother,
grandmother, brother and sister. Only I survived
to die again. The top of the shop
where we used to live is still fire-chewed, hollow,
no roof, nothing. Only the bottom has been dolled up,

painted a yellow brighter than the heart
of the sun. I stand awhile and watch people pour
in and out. And then I walk in. It's as though nothing
happened. Conscious Music. The Rasta clerk
behind the mesh springs up when he sees me
enter, and someone kills the music and suddenly
I'm six again and learning how to smoke
in the shop while everyone is asleep upstairs
and I'm forgetting to snuff out the candles
and cigarette and falling asleep on the floor
and waking up to the house on fire as the night
sinks in flames and I feel myself running,
running out on fire and half-believing
that I'm still in a dream, jumping into
the well behind the house and crying
and screaming until screaming men show up
for water to douse the house. But it is too
late. It is always too late. The sun falls
asleep and to my surprise the street lights come
on. I turn around now, because nobody knows
what really happened that burning night.
I'm just an old boy, walking back
into a new light, learning to forgive God.

THE DEPORTED

From the plane Jamaica looks
like a loaded gun. He wants to tell
the U.S. Marshals flanking him
that it's like being flown back into a grave,
he decides when they land and the heat
is insufferable and the cement sky
reminds him of the cell he called
home in the U.S. for the last
five years. Freedom smells
like jerk chicken and urine and gasoline.
He walks into the Caribbean
Sea until the sea lifts him into her arms
and rocks him. His aunt picks
him up and brings him back
to his childhood house, a concrete box
on concrete stilts overlooking a flood-happy
gully. He bends to go under the doorway
after taking in the bush town. He closes
his eyes and imagines entering his wife back
in Connecticut. He leaves the house without
opening his eyes and climbs down the thirteen
front steps as blind as he used to do as a child.
He opens his eyes when he slips and begins to fly
and catches himself before shattering his wrists
and glasses. Thirteen years ago when he left for good
he didn't have glasses. Now he feels like a god
in hell. Everything rises with the hearty wind,
the bloody cries of farm animals, the giant Jamaican
flag, his spirit. Cars die in potholes. The single-story
All Age School looks like an old derailed train.
Nobody remembers him. Not even the sun.
But everybody knows his crime. He sees it

reflected in their every scorn. But he's no O.J.
He simply plunged guilt into his wife's
lover and it nearly killed him.
The local women are ripe, bountiful and ready
to be picked. The colorful shops and houses
fire up his heart. White churches live on
every corner. An apple vendor in the square gives
him a cloudy smile for speaking the Queen's
high English. The grass says green all year
as a family of palm trees wave
to him. When the sun remembers him,
he feels more hope than he can conquer.

MONA OF SEAVIEW GARDENS, JAMAICA

She's tired of being entered
like a church, sweetening the bitter
lives of men. The married man inside
her now is the fire-and-brimstone-preaching
local pastor. He ransacks
her body, knocking over her fan. She thanks
God she has a view of the sun-stroked
Caribbean Sea, so her mind can travel
out her bedroom window over gunshots
and single-story, halved, faux-bricked
ghetto houses with zinc roofs. She imagines
taking a naked dip in the sea, entering
it and becoming as wide and deep, able
to absorb all her johns at once.
When her mind returns she sees
the pastor studying her like his Bible,
complimenting her blonde wig, her brown
skin, her starved figure. She nods
and waits for him to expire in her,
the way he loves it. He's as awkward as a bear
but the weight of him is no burden. She thinks
of her two solemn children, needing
schoolbags, school clothes, bullet-proof
vests, but he doesn't seem
to want to finish. He's happy inside
her, the way she can recline in the sea
for hours at night after a day like this.

Finally happiness drains from his
face and fills her with relief. It's Sunday
and he's expected in church. He leaves her two
Nannies on the dresser. She used to ask
heaven for forgiveness until a john called
her heaven. Now she can't ignore the endless
church bells stinging her at noon.

MAY PEN

A fire catches over May Pen as thick
and brightening as a hustler's fake jewelry.
Our country bus guns like a dog down crowded streets
of market stalls, and people painted black with shadows
of medium rise bakeries and Churches of God. Freed
school boys in desert-colored suits with craters
of pimples stamped like potholes in their sun-hot faces
board at the clock tower. A school of sea-blue uniformed girls
flood in behind with their river scents and chemically
straightened hair, girls who sit on boys already seated,
who fit comfortably down like the ring I keep
pulling up and down around my finger. The clock
bell rings in the head of the stone tower like the memory
of how long ago my wife was one of these loving
girls bouncing in the heart of my lap as we bumped
over tin-shack-sided roads black with protest up
through dreams of green-leafy mountains falling
before heaven.

SESTINA TO PATRICIA

I have housed you in my mind these years
across acres of time and shiny ocean stillness
that merged old age and new innocence.
How you swung hands with me, my love,
the island was summer and we were young
after school on a Friday afternoon, a light breeze,

a moment unfolding in the fluttering breeze
shedding your school-blue uniform, only thirteen years
into your life, kissing me wildly, the young
birds chirping from shady alders, my fingers stilled
electric nerves on your cool night skin, with love
taking you one step further from your innocence.

Time and tears flooding our innocence
I left you unsung songs in the island breeze
scattering our feelings into a family of fallen leaves. My love
of Jamaica, unlove of America, two aging worlds, years
of cold, warm days, oceans apart, our time still,
ageless, locked away in the sunful days of youth.

This day finds you older, decades past your youth,
a matron, housed in warm incense,
wrestling life and petting boredom, in a still
and lonely countryside, tempted by evening's sultry breeze,
to rebuke the cries of your children and dream back years
into hours of riverbed loving.

The grass is golden in my mind. I dig for love
and hope green springs and fresh memories make you young
again, once a scene unfurls in your mind, summer years,
the way the swaying trees giggled, we mocked innocence—
two bodies bonding, sounds knocking on the breeze,
the world rocking until the moment rocking still.

I have collected your dimpled smiles, braided hair—still
photos into a tearful lake, and love?
Love can exist this way, framed alive with ease
along a stream squinting sunlight into the eyes of young
lovers and jasmines burn their lives for incense.
I have ordained you a Goddess, exalting you for years,

and praying, praying that the running years can be still
like innocence and you may not leave my stay, Patricia,
until the ripe old sun falls into our riverbed days.

BAPTISM

At seven I wanted to be born
again. My rebirth took place under
an old train bridge at dawn. The water
reached over my head and so the pastor
had to hold me up as the crowd
clapped and sang on the wide stony
bank. "A child shall lead us," he belted
out and dipped me. When I rose
I felt like God's son.

SUNDAYS, TROUT HALL, JAMAICA

Sundays were often brighter
before and after church.
During church—a long, white, cavelike
structure at the right end
of the commons—the football field
waited on us; the clay cricket
pitch hardened in the sun. Sam's unstolen
oranges continued to ripe over
the barks of patrolling dogs as ungodly
boys sat in the forbidden hands
of apple trees. The gully continued to die
of thirst. Cows chewed on. Penned
at one end of the All Age School, hogs
hollered out to be fed or freed; canes
waved for us around them, birds dined on
our plums and mangoes. Soon we hoped
the brown-spotted preacher'd wrap his sermon
up and we'd head home
to find our hard-boiling peas,
soft as our brain-washed hearts.

SKY BEER

His daughter gets pregnant and everybody
thinks it's his, because he's Sky Beer. He's never
washed nor combed his hair (he's mildly
Rastafarian) and lives on a sliver of land
not high enough over the gully. When it rains
he's always an hour or two away
from being washed away in his sleep, no less.
Sky and his daughters, Chant, 16, and April,
12, sleep in the same room but never in the same
bed, and Chant's been pregnant now one
month and Sky hasn't chugged a beer in three
months because he can't afford to, so it couldn't
be his, he could never have done it sober. How he hates
when Sunday rises over the white, grave-gripped
Church of God and all the good Christians ejaculate
from their concrete box houses and stream to church
in sharp black suits and sun-catching white dresses.
He wishes it would rain and stay night forever. God can't hear
the way the thirsty goats behind the sunny All Age
School weep and bleat at the merciless sun, nor
can He hear Chant and April snoring in the zinc
behind, nor can He see Sky Beer about to jump, all the way
down to the stony dry-season gully and break open
his head like a dry coconut. He's not afraid of death. Death is
sleep and wake up in his own world. And death isn't
ugly, death is that leggy browning down
near the cardboard church with HIV, too. Death is Sky Beer
asking Chant who the baby's father is and her saying nobody
and him wanting to strangle her, but fighting death instead.
He hasn't had a drink in so long. Now he's tossing
down Red Stripes and tossing the bottles at the gully;
you ought to see the sounds they make

and don't make when he hurls them into the deep
heart of the pool just under the bridge down
from the coffee field across from the rich white homes
with satellites and cherry trees. But he could never desert
Jamaica to slave on apple farms abroad to afford satellites
and lengthen his house. No. He will
never do what his mother and father did:
left him a boy with his dying Grandmother to fly
abroad and never returning, neither of them (mother
flew to England to be a nanny and his daddy
flew to Florida to pick oranges and apples.)
Nor will he work for Mr. Sharke, the snowy Englishman,
in his Ugli factory and not because Sky's only just over five
feet tall and would have trouble reaching
Uglies, those grainy green-skinned football-sized fruits, hybrid
offspring of tangerines and oranges, are as corrupt as kids
left behind by foreign-going fathers. Who impregnated
Chant when Sky Beer can't even afford zinc
for his house? Mostly he does work with his tractor
which is parked out near the scarred main road.
He had to buy new zinc for the house when it
washed away last time. His wife, Willi, is gone now,
not dead, but she tramped back to live
with her mother, because he loved
to beat her in the rain so much. Especially
on Sundays to show the Christians crossing
the bridge now how much he doesn't care
about God. Think about it. In 5000 years
people are going to look down on us
for believing in heaven and hell. Hell and Heaven is
America, where money grows on farms and the Man
loves to hold you down. He's not afraid of being

called stupid, undersexed and dangerous; he's more
afraid of not being who he wants to be while
other people can be who they want to be.
He wants to be God, his own God.
He was born before Jamaica was born.
He knows how England treated Jamaica rotten
over the years before Independence;
a lot of people have forgotten that because look
how Jamaicans kill each other and the gays
in the name of God. Listen to that tractor fucking
up the land over the commons to build a new
missionary church that will kill twilight. He has no trouble
loving another man if love is love.
Sometimes he finds things and brings them
back but people think he's a thief. Last week
a goat wandered into his kitchen and Sky Beer
marched him back to Monsieur Mather and now
everybody keeps an eye out for him.
There never used to be a barbed wire
fence on one side of him until his now dead pigs
used to run all over the grounds of the peach All
Age School. Now if there's a storm
he has to risk cutting off his head going under
the sharp spiky wires or else run up
the narrow path overlooking the high
speeding gully, knowing that one slip
and he's gone forever. But you want to know
how he got his name. Sky Beer was down in the square
one night. Reggae music pounding. He was drunk
and dancing and then it started to drizzle
and the drizzle tasted like beer and he couldn't
believe it and so he shouted, "Sky Beer, Sky

Beer," to everyone but no one believed him
but they all started calling him Sky Beer.
But what does he care? What does he care what
this salty world thinks of him? "Sky Beer, Sky Bear."
Even the little ones taunt him. He scares them and they
run but the big ones laugh in his eyes. The death of respect
is death. He wants to cut off his dreads but can't.
His daughters even call him Sky when they are mad.
Who will raise the living from the dead? To jump,
he simply moves closer to the edge, and never
looking down, lets go of his worries, but he doesn't
die; no, he manages to land on spongy wet sand
and only his ankles radiate with pain. Lying up,
he knows now he can only fall so far. Death is no longer
in love with him. So if he's not God, then who is?
It's Chant and April crying over him.

New Haven, Connecticut, USA:
Between Dreams

400 YEARS LATER

"Thanks for not profiling me," my bumper sticker wails
at cops trailing me through heavenly neighborhoods. I am tall,
black and Jamaican. Not a bear. I don't have a relationship
with guns or weed. I drive a sheepish cloud-gray
Buick with no blinding chrome rims through America.
Sometimes racism stalks me in departmental stores, too,
like a horror movie demon. Sometimes it runs away
from me at night. It smiles at me on trains. I love black
women and white women and every color
in between, but mostly I love breasts. I believe breasts
prove there is a God. I wear orange shirts to work
on gloomy days. I bleed friends. I'm getting
a divorce and it feels a lot like getting out of prison
though I've never been locked up. Sometimes America
feels like a cage. Like being homeless at home.
Like being banished to the deserted island of the living room
couch. My future ex-wife was an atheistic, moon-white
hippie. I don't have a monster cock. I have a Christian
heart and a stormy relationship with God. I'm a barely employed
Employment Specialist, future Social Worker, past devil.
Sometimes I overdose on porn. Sometimes I overdose on hope
while dreaming of a planet called Equality. I love to devirginize
the beach at dawn, sand hugging my toes,
　　a chain of cars on the avenue. I love music
in my bloodstream, not alcohol. I love dream-
inducing songs called "3 a.m." at 1 p.m. I don't live
in the hood, but I love to walk in the hood without fear of being
crucified by a bullet. I'm not yet buried in prison. I wish
　　we would hurry
up and bury the N-word. I'm a slave to money,
sex, freedom and opportunity, but I love soul to soul
conversations deep into an oven night,

with a scarred black woman who dares me to worship her. I say,
"I feel like we're still in slavery and you just got whipped
with insults and it's my job to bandage your confidence."
I say, "You're not a ho." I say, "You're heaven," kissing hell away.
"You're a warm river in my childhood." I'm working on
    my relationship
with time. I'm patient, but my anger is a leaking dam. Sometimes
my speech impediment blocks my heart. I love my music loud
and my silence deep. I don't hate the police, but I don't trust
a demigod with the green light to kill. Yes, I don't live in the hood,
but I love to walk through the hood to see what the media
forgets: kids playing hopscotch in the chirping shade,
ambulances idling, the wind combing through the afros
of oaks, love music like sea breeze, hearts beating
to bouncing basketballs, a cocktail of voices, marijuana clouds,
grills smoking, renovated red houses wearing the sun
like a crown, black goddesses in yellow booty
shorts, cops roaming like coyotes, kids tossing
around the N-word like a baseball, 400 years later.

STARING AT THIRTY

My cell's dead again. It's Jesus's
birthday. I can't find my charger. I tear the house
apart as thirty stares at me like a tiger
on the cover of a wildlife magazine. Listening
to Kanye West charges my ego. The impotent
Connecticut sun licks up the meager offering
of snow as light and shade sumo-wrestle
in the living room. The world's still
a beautiful woman. My wife's in love
with her new job and dreams. I'm in love
with a sultry country. But jobless, can't fly.
Turning up the heat, I ogle Jamaica
on the Travel Channel like a faithful husband
at a strip club. My neighbor's white
cat lounges on my porch like the promise
of more snow, watching me fish
my charger from the belly of the sofa. I see Mother's
trying to call me from Jamaica, but I think
I don't need to pick up. My cell chirps, I close
my eyes and again I'm a boy growing in the still
Jamaican countryside, inhaling the perfumy scents
of uncleaned pigpens, devouring graveyard mangoes,
tripping through the green blur of woodlands,
swimming in bottomless rivers. "In forty
years," Mother told me twenty years
ago, "You will look back at life like Lot's wife."
"I'm twenty-nine and haven't made any angels
to plunder presents beneath the Christmas tree,"
I keep apologizing to my pastor, who keeps
repeating, "Nonsense. Nonsense. God, it's all
Nonsense, brother. Pray. Young black
brother. Pray." But my life is an unheard prayer. I step

outside and talk back to the lonely Long Island
Sound, ignoring its ungodly breath. At night
Long Island looks like a fire-chewed
cigarette from West Haven. Now the sun's a baby
in a crib of clouds. When the wind
begins to touch me like a cold mistress, my future
ex-wife wakes and her hair lights the day.

HOW DO I LOOK?

It takes only a moment for the Polaroid
to be born: my mother standing not
in our concrete orange house in Jamaica
but in her bosses' living room in a white church
dress taking pictures for me to take back
to Bro, Sis and Dad and his light
new wife in America. This is Hopedale,
Canada melting. The rich black
and white kids she's babysitting erupt now
and again from where they're watching cartoons
in the TV room. I aim the house camera.
"I am a prisoner with no green
card," Mother is saying as I snap.
"80 dollars for the whole week. God
Knows." She unwrinkles her face
into happiness for another shot.
"How I look?" Mother asks as I
watch the picture form. A gilded
portrait of the boss, a black engineer, somehow
got into the shot. Of course, having been
staying in this cloud-gray manor for the last
few days I know Mother is in love
with this plump, bald-headed man with a corporate
smirk. I tear up the picture and make sure
to put the pieces in my pocket, careful
to not let the cruel woman of the house
know we used her camera. I steer Mother
further from the man and closer to the table of blue
china. "That one was sad," I tell her. "Okay
then," she intones. Fluffing her gloomy hair,
she walks into a painting of what looks like an island
in blood-yellow lava by a silver-green sea. Smiling,

I lower the camera, look through the white
curtains across the eyesore pond to make
sure her bosses aren't driving up into the yard
and into the picture. "How I look now?" she says,
smiling on me. "Like God's bride," I say as swans
land on the pond and snow flurries
dissolve in my fear of drowning.

MAN OVERBOARD

We're not on a ship, but I feel
like a man overboard when the boss
hands out pink slips and tells us
we're laid off. Half my life I've worked
in this workshop, shaping slaughtered
trees into store racks and now I'm being
sent to drift in a mindless world.
Outside, the reality of the sun
hits like a board over
my bald head, and although I had been fully
expecting to sink into the ground
once I took my first outdoor steps
as an unemployed man, I am buoyed
by the fact that my feet hit solid ground.

SAD HOUSE

I cut the silence into clean slices
of bread on the counter. The sun
winks on the knife. I turn the pipe
on and leave it on for its thundering music
on plates in the sink. My soon-to-be
ex-wife lurks somewhere in the house.
In the bedroom or the bathroom
or the basement. She's a tornado
of silence. Our faded yellow house cannot see
the sea, but we can feel its mad power
every time the wind wrestles the house.
When she emerges from the basement
she is white and I am black. Her browned hair
coils at my stare like a snake. Her eyes
have lost their light for me. We regard
each other, like the first man and woman.

EX-WIFE

To…fall in love with the sadness of another.
—Billy Collins

I fell in love with your sadness, not your chameleon
eyes, not the unfinished tattoo of the giant turtle
crawling up your back, not the twin snakes mating
around your ankles, not the black tree of knowledge
on your white shoulders, not the permanent love note
to your suicidal dead ex on your collarbone, not the weeping
roses on your wrist, not the storm of your hair, not
the moment my trembling hand freed your buried
breasts. Yes, I fell in love with the lonely silences between
your words, with the fact that your two younger, prettier
sisters had wedded their souls to their soul
mates while you were finding yourself after being lost
in drugs, alcohol and depression, that you loved children
though you could never give birth to nothing
but moodiness, that you lived in a big empty
house and worked three jobs to support it like a child,
that you lived near a sea you couldn't see, that you had adopted
a blind sea turtle named George you had never seen,
that your evil sisters had kids that looked like you, that you
drove a gray bug that was too small for you, that one
had to search for your beauty like flowers in a forest,
that you had forgotten how to laugh, that you were in love
with erasing my black pain, that your father
had inadvertently made you into an angry tomboy,
that your mother loved her dogs more than you, that you
loved men who hated to love you, that hard drugs
had eaten a quarter of your brain, that you loved to question
your sanity, that you had scoliosis and an iron
rod for a spine, that you had infinite back pain which you
soothed with cannabis, that you always feared death would

send you cancer, that you told me how a guy once left you
out of an orgy, that you cried whenever you spoke
about your uncle who passed away alone in a rainy cabin
in the heart of Maine, that all your exes were either dead
or in rehab, that you were allergic to tropical birds, dust, bees,
sunlight and sweet men.

INTERRACIAL PORN

The kettle whistles like a hardworking man.
A naked woman stands over a counter, pretending
to butter bread, her skin white and ominous as rain
clouds, her hair red and stormy. The camera zooms
to the moon dripping milky light on a black car pulling
into the driveway. A black man is coming
home from a hard night of work. When he gets inside
the house he unbuckles his carpenter's tool belt,
walks up behind her and plugs himself dreamily into her.
For a moment she pretends she doesn't know
what's going on. She has this shocked look on her face
as though she were being abducted. She squeals.
He has a bricky body. She rinses her finger in his mouth.
The man wants to scream. The TV clothes them in
light-brown prairie light as they fall to the hardwood floor.
They give each other hell, then heaven.

DIVORCE

The spring sun is heartbreakingly
cold. Sick cars sound like healthy
trucks and healthy trucks like low
planes. The skunky Long Island
Sound tosses like an insomniac
assailed by impotent light. The disembodied
beat of a basketball on concrete jolts
my heart. Drunk on porn, club-grinding
and heartbreak, I devirginize the beach
with each step, sand mugging my toes. The wind
stings like betrayal. Back in the parking lot,
my car waits for me like a horse.

THE REFORMED RACIST

While we drink, I tell the reformed
racist that I'm scared to hell he'll push me
off this third floor balcony into the black
as me night below and he laughs,
"I'm afraid you will too." We stare
at the winkless stars, still sipping beer.
The wind carries up the voice
of the street. The clouds are cotton-white
though it's night. A shoe hangs like a man
from a live wire. The reformed racist
is taller and crazier than me. I say
it's like holding back a lion, your feelings.
He said it's like keeping the lawn low.

AS A BOY IN THE INSANE ASYLUM
IN HARTFORD, CT

One boy here looks like Brad
Pitt and all the girls go crazier
for him. He says he will fuck
the crazy out of them when
he gets out of here and they
get out of here. He has a habit of fingering
his blonde hair and widening his baby-blue
eyes while rubbing his concrete abs.
"Everywhere I go it's like this," he says.
"Girls hunting me. I can fuck any girl
I want." "Isn't that heaven then?" I say. "Why
are you here?" He says he lost happiness
when his girlfriend broke his heart which broke
his mind. Now he's only faithful to drugs.
He says his ex was more beautiful
than the most beautiful woman
I can imagine. I imagine Jamaica
because I'm Jamaican. He says she's
more paradise than paradise. We stand
at the barred window at the end
of the hallway. The ultra-bright light
in the building is like a cloudy day. Dark
buries the light outside. Brad is wearing
a green shirt though it's fall. Kids hearing
voices scream through their locked
rooms behind us. We feel pretty lucky
to sort of have our sanity. "Why
you here?" he says. "I don't know,"
I say. "I think I'm an artist." I'm taller
than Brad and so I search over his head
through a window to a car's headlights
burning through the buried city.

I KNEW I LOVED YOU WHEN YOU
TOLD ME YOU HAD CANCER

I knew I loved you when
you told me you
had cancer and I told you
I would kill death. You smiled
and the parking lot filled
with light. The wind
fingered your wig, your face
forlorn as a cliff, your skin
pale as a bright day, your eyes
red clouds, your voice
and tears dammed. The sun
didn't owe us everything. I saw
your words as a strange river
of sharks. I wanted to throw
my life between yours and death
by kissing you. But you were in love
with a broken marriage, bulging
with his angel. You looked me in the eye
and did not feed my longing. We hugged.
Your heart thundered and I felt the flow
of life in your veins, your summer-in-winter
warmth and I knew you wouldn't leave
this world without a war.

NAVINA

Night in your hair, day in your smile,
faraway places in your voice, a raining
village in Germany, the Seine slithering
through Paris, quietly humming neon
signs in Tokyo, a leafy sun waking
over a garrulous Indian market. Something
about the way you speak with your eyes
resurrects my lost mother's love, my love
of Jamaica, my faith in heaven on earth.
Your perennially dark jeans against
tropical skin, your ethereal dresses like fog
wrapping what I someday hope
to witness to know your warmth.

KYRA

"Early in the morning, late in the century."
—Zadie Smith, *White Teeth*

Early in the century, late in the morning
here you are a songbird without a song,
in a yellow breakfast nook called
the Pantry, across from a man smelling
like flowers, your hair long and natural
unlike your unnatural history. Orphaned at birth
to an Italian family now your world, the Ivy
education in your voice, the horses you grew
up riding for sport, the wine you drink to block
your road-not-taken past, your face, a sunny
lake tossed by a manic breeze. I find peace
in your black beauty. I believe in a God
when you look into my eyes; your smile,
the light of the year. Your voice turns
from a dammed lake to a summer river
to a midnight sea. I'm engulfed
in your words. You're a bright day
at the beach with no chance of rain. The world
shuttles us on. When you tell me I'm handsome,
it's the law. When you tell me I should be confident,
I'm confidence, molding us into one.

FREDERICK-DOUGLASS KNOWLES

[For a Friend named after Frederick Douglass]

Last night, I stood in the mirror and saw
your face, ten years older, the dark cotton
fields of history written in your dark-white stubbles,
a hat cocked on your head like men in the early Jim
Crow era, black people hanging from fruit trees
and yet we kill each other. My friend and fellow poet,
right now cops comb the darkness of the *Elm City*
for the killer of another black son like us with ditches
of worry lines worrying his forehead. Whoever speaks
with guns is a son of violence. Crowned with the name
Frederick-Douglass from birth you learned to convert
the weight of expectations into love and light.
Professor of black studies, you teach and preach
the trail of our pain, exhuming the tortured
lives of our ancestors to give voice to their cries,
the slaves who leapt from ships into the deadly
arms of the Atlantic, those chained in the sweltering
wombs of ships, those with signatures of whips
across their backs, those lighting a movement
up from slavery. The stage loves you and your voice
transports the people to a time when the N-word
meant hate, to a time now when we endeavor to embody
the dream, to shine words on injustice. I hear Frederick Douglass,
I hear Malcolm, I hear King, I hear Moses. In your voice,
I hear the only way forward is backwards towards
a time when slave ships gave birth to slaves
on the shores of the new world. How many
suns have we sat in cafés in the *Heartbeat*

and the *Elm City* mining the racist soul of America
in soulful poems ending in a bleak past and a bright
future? Now you're turning forty and turning away
from the old you. Four hundred years later we are free
to try to be free. In the mirror, my face bears
a smile as the past works in us.

MEGHAN

It's no secret, but I find peace in the green
night of your owl-large eyes. They reflect
nothing and are beautiful for it like cathedral
windows in a storm. The constant
sunrise of your smile, your knowing face regal
as a queen's, your dark bangs drumming silkily
against the drum of your forehead. You have a voice
like the arrival of spring. Your touch is a butterfly,
your fragrance, a forgotten garden in my childhood.
I love your ethereal wit, how you're forever going on
about your brief turbulent affair with New York
City, your victory over anorexia. Your empathy
for the plants you eat. I love how you only believe
in heaven on earth. Yet you're the heaven you don't
believe in. Something about the way you are
always dressed in delicate designer clothes makes you
seem as vulnerable as a vase about to tumble
off a glass-topped coffee table, in a house bounced
by a passing train. I have dreamt of catching
you single ever since you told me you were in love
with that chef who hated your cat. I love how
you are forever nursing nostalgia for places I will
never meet, that you are as mysterious as that phrase
"true happiness" and sometimes obliquely mean,
though mostly summer sweet. When you speak
I want to never fall asleep as I think of mountains
and streams cutting through mountains, lonely,
but flowing ever still beneath wind-strummed
leaves, birds crisscrossing an indifferent sky.

TRISHA

Our spirits melded on the dance
floor like we were born
to be each other. You held me
like a dying man, like
a newborn, whispering
life into my ear: love-scarred,
black mother, master's in Psychology,
God-fearing, dubbed Oreo
for speaking moon-white, a son crowned
Prince. You are more beautiful
than Jamaica, more paradise
than paradise, a heart like the sun, sweeter
than vacation, a voice sunny
with intelligence, compassion, cooler
than every spring. In summer we moved
through the world like a revolution,
transforming each other into happiness. Your smile
flowers; your touch, a resurrection. Your laughter
rang my desire. Your thundering hips swayed
to the music of your heels. At dinner above
the Omni Hotel, New Haven staring up at us,
your anger was love. You swore I was nicer
than a warm day in winter, your Jamaica
in America, since I'm Jamaican, a social
worker half-way through grad school,
shackled by the dam of a speech
impediment. Your touch freedom,
we dove into heart-to-hearts about black
love and black pain, how you felt like a Goddess
without worshippers. How we medicate
with materialism. I loved you, but you
could never return it, as winter leapt
fall and broke the spell of your warmth.

CATHERINE

That lone birthmark on your right
cheek is an island I long to visit
with my lips. In class on a rainy
night, your hair a silent waterfall
fanning darkly over a stubborn head
and rocky shoulders, crashing
into my senses. Your bottomless intelligence,
pie-sweet voice. Angel, social worker
in the making. Your laughter kills
gloom. Eyes forever widening
with empathy, you empower where
there is no light. Weekends you live
in books. I am moved by your Restless
Leg Syndrome, the way you must beat music
into a hard-as-your-life floor with tiny heels as rain
pings and reclines on the roof. Short
beauty. Your voice is a hit song
I can't shake. I hear your boyfriend felt
gold when he found you. I've seen you
look into my eyes and I felt blind, the terror
of your past. The seizures like earthquakes
reshaping your reality. Born a mother.
Babysitting your per diem mother as she kills
time with Sam Lights. Your beloved twin brother
buried in an asylum. How you dumped your closet
racist ex. How my over the cliff sense of humor
shocks you into adorable cartoonish faces that cover
turmoil. You have a heart like the sun,
I once told you, and your smile was all
sunrise warming the face of the world.

STRIPPERS

They walk like penguins,
in heels, wounded, and flightless.
Say no to a lap dance special
and it triggers an avalanche
of shame. They are humans,
after all. The music is the blood
of the scene. They have names
like Molly and Saturn. So much
beauty. It makes you think
of otherworldly New England falls,
all those blondes and browns
and black rosy black skies. One
stripper is manic and reminds you
of a runaway train with you
in it. She calls you her brother
and licks your furry shoes. Another
stripper named Lilly is so innocent
and easily wounded she could be
your lost daughter.

STRIPPER IN GLASSES

Her body is a black garden
of tattoos, a rose
cries petals down
her waist and legs to a pool
of light on top of her
foot as the music thunders
and patrons tornado in
marijuana clouds. Another
tattoo of moonlight speaks
to sunlight on her stomach
mapped with birthmarks
as she coils and swings onstage
naked as the approaching
day. Someone pours money
and drinks on her braids
and she pauses to clean
her intellectual black
glasses with her little sleeveless
jean jacket, which she uses
to conceal her too small
breasts. When she shakes out
her hair and puts on her
glasses you see something
of the librarian or corporate
business woman in her
movements. Her eyes back,
she skies and smiles like someone's
little daughter at Christmas.
She snakes around the pole
and launches onto a man,
wraps her beauty around
him, while his eyes bulge

with this goddess attached
to his sorrows. His money flies
out of his hand and flutters
around them like a hit bird's
feathers. She opens up herself
to him and he stares inside her
and kisses her rose. She freezes
when the journey of the song
is over and kneels down
to collect her bread.

I NO LONGER HAD A SPEECH IMPEDIMENT

Last night, I dreamt I no longer had a speech
impediment and I couldn't stop talking,
like that warm river in my childhood which drowned
so many of my friends and carries in its voice
their souls to this day. All languages were light.
All words were lies. When I was sad, I couldn't stop
crying about nothing. I couldn't stop believing
in peace, love and racial harmony. I couldn't stop
driving through traffic lights without worries
and accidents and the cops chasing me, couldn't stop
chasing me though they couldn't stop me. It makes
sense. It started to rain and it didn't stop. The sun
woke up and couldn't stop licking up the rain.
We went to war again and couldn't stop going
to wars until the world was ours, even the parts
we couldn't stop hating. I loved all people and couldn't
stop loving all people and I wanted to wake up
but couldn't wake up and so I went on dreaming,
even in the real world.

NEWHALLVILLE, NEW HAVEN

I dreamt I won the lottery, but couldn't
find the ticket like Emancipation. I woke to another
absent sun like my father. Mother had left the house warm
by leaving the oven on. I left the house to explore
a day with no shape. Our hood was a goldmine
for funeral homes and Yale studies, as police cars
and ambulances stung like lightning
at every corner. Kids pushed kids in strollers as guns
spoke to guns. People resembled their crumbling, peeling
houses beneath anesthetic marijuana clouds. We were buried
in prison and on the corner. Color was the unbreakable chain
spring or Obama's ascension couldn't break. We stumbled home
from prison chained to our records, locked
out of jobs. Crack found lost souls. A drug dealer in shades
doled out drugs to ruined psyches like any good
doctor. A neighbor painted her house forest-green
and it attracted sunlight and gunshots. A dog barked
away winter. We medicated with sex, church and the N-word,
too. Cars with blinding rims showered us with music. In summer
the girls wore nothing and everyone felt cloudy on a sunny
day as Newhallville and The Yale Science Park biotech
complex faced each other like bulls needing to lock horns.

LYNNETTE

As my Malibu waved a white flag of smoke
under a bridge heavy with thundering
traffic, you modeled along. You seemed formed
out of the cool night, your clear night skin, your leopard
blouse, your bark tight jeans, your smile, headlights,
your dreads thriving in winter, your heels knocking
at the lonely house of my heart. I said, "My car is trouble."
You said, "That stinks." I will forever be glued
to your velvet handshake. Your lips a wound I wanted
to bandage with kisses. I left my car
and we wedding-walked to the little cottage-like
restaurant, where you were the featured poetry
reader. You twirled the audience around
your finger with poems about what it meant
to be a conscious black goddess in America. You looked
like Lauryn Hill, wrote like Maya Angelou. You had a voice
like a violin, like heartwarming drizzle
on tin roof, a voice mixed with the waterfall voices
of our ancestors. You shook with orgasmic
thrill as your poems left you. And then we gravitated
back to our lives. You nursed Springfield. I fed New
Haven jobs. You conceived an angel and I was consumed
with a love that would never bloom in Connecticut.
You moonlighted as the Oprah of Facebook, posting
probing questions about why happiness eluded
you like a squirrel. I didn't only dream of us making love
like the first fire. I dreamt of us plugging into
the shocking racist soul of America in deep all night
conversations, our world woolled in snow; my body,
your blanket; your smile, my sunrise.

THE HEAVEN BEYOND WHAT WE
KNOW OF HEAVEN

We lie on the deserted island of your couch
like survivors after a lifetime of shipwrecks,
the voices of the TV and traffic clashing like titan
waves. A movie about cowboys battling aliens watches
us as does the one-eyed pirate moon through the picture
frame window, your cool night skin littered with stars
of scars, like a slave. I try to touch each scar away
like waves on trampled sand. We talk about bandaging
confidence, how you're the heaven beyond
what we know of heaven. Your fragrance the Caribbean
Sea, your smile moonlight, your natural hair
a perfect storm on my horizon. My heart, your heartbreak,
we dig into the future and the future of the past. How
I can't kiss you or enter your world because my marriage
is still on life support. But I play you like a piano,
and you are the music.

CLUB

The liquor smells like body
odor. The music punches your senses
as the DJ implores you to go out
of your mind. A statute of a medieval suit
of armor and a statue of Predator guards
the bar. Colorful lights chase each other
around like puppies. All the women look
like dolled up goddesses. Say you just got
divorced and feel as free as spring.
"There are so many women
in here," the DJ sighs. "They need
 you to not be shy." He darkens
the darkened lights and amorous
smoke fills the club. "I'm on that good
kush and alcohol," thunders from the speakers.
"Long as my bitches love me," the song
continues. A woman in nothing
but a white bikini grinds on
you while it rains.

ODE TO LAKE WHITNEY, A RESERVOIR

Friend, like you, I have a speech
impediment, which blocks my heart
and shutters my mind. You flow
smooth as hate; rain tickles your back
as you toss and turn in your prison
bed. You are forever pregnant with hope.
Trees dress and undress before you. Birds
preen in your restless mirror as the wind
pushes you to punch and punch the dam.

THE CLUB BOUNCER

A living statue, he watches drunk
goddesses dance like forbidden fruits in the music
of wind-strummed leaves. The DJ's voice rips
into his trance like thunder. A strawberry
blond in an orange dress
dances into his dream where he peels
her dress and enters her world. A lost dancer
spills perfumy beer on his face, black shirt,
black pants. A black girl in a white dress, red, white
and black sky-high heels backs into his invisibility.
He's dying to head home and exorcise
his dreams. He backs away and tries to forget
that her body had felt like his orthopedic bed,
like times as a boy when he'd wake and sneak
onto a doggy apple orchard, bite
into apples, without picking them.

ANOTHER GUN SPEAKS

Another gun speaks and transports
another black man to heaven or hell,
or wherever we go when our hearts
explode at two in the morning, after
a night of heavenly clubbing while
the killers become night and the drum
of bullets slackens and dies and the Siren
of the de-souled black man wails, "Do something,
do something" to the crowd as cops emerge
like lions from the crowd, sprinting towards
the scene at the intersection of love and hate,
as the moon-kissed woman, in white heels
and a black starry dress, kneels down
to touch her man's forehead like Jesus,
shrieking, "Get up Sam," but knowing
we are living in King's nightmare.

MIDNIGHT PROMISES

"Call now to eliminate black pain," the midnight
infomercial promises. Ditsy with sleep, I squint
at the blurry words on the mute TV, hop out
of bed to fetch my glasses. No. It really says,
"Eliminate back pain." I fall back to earth.
Climb downstairs. Down a beer. I don't
think of angels when it snows at night.
I think of ashes. I think of slaves and the voices
of slaves in my voice. I think of my soul
as the wailing hull of a Middle Passage
ship. I know I'm not in a dream
when the beer bottle escapes my hand
and crashes to the floor. We're living in King's
aborted dream. The couch looks like a warm
woman. I lie down. Can't find the remote
to change my life. But the TV's all fireworks.
Mute too. The president waves to me
from the podium. I clap. America still stings.
But unabridged pain doesn't know me right now.

FROM THE NEW HAVEN GREEN

The sunny Yale students interrupt traffic
to cross the one way street between
cavernous Gothic buildings, to class, to Barnes
and Noble, to the square under the Green's
trees by the ageless handsome brown and white
churches with their dead tower clocks. The uneven
skyscrapers resemble some homeless man's
teeth. The park benches are worn down with the smell
of sleep. Some hours unseen
clock tower bells ring together; three turtling city
buses arrive at the same time going
the same way and the crowd at the glass bus stop
scurry like ants to fill them. There's the persistent sound
of drilling that never quite leaves you. The African hawks
fake gold watches in front of the Blue Nile
and Expressions clothing stores. Near-naked, white
couples sunbathe on The Green. On the steps
of the United Illuminating Company an olive
woman sits rocking her baby doll madly.
A ranting police dog drives her away; in cloudy
bars drunk residents pronounce New Haven
New Heaven and circling birds shy away
from that one old tree, across from the three-story
library, which has failed to grow back
this spring. There's the smell of exhaust
everywhere as the sun goes down in Starbucks.
And nights, when the traffic is especially thick
around The Green, the homeless, hearing the
highways call from a hidden distance,
can feel imprisoned in this state as gunshots
erupt from headache neighborhoods.

NEW HAVEN

The city has a voice with jackhammers, Yale
kids, homeless preachers, non-profits, turtling buses,
sirens and gunshots in it. In West River, flowers grow
out of murders. In Westville, Victorians, speed bumps,
blooming cherry trees pretty as brides. Around the Green, students
and one-way traffic clog the heart of the city. A statue of Cicero
sitting guard, the giant, columned courthouse stands unsteady
as a poisoned King, the library its overshadowed brother.
The sun rides the uneven high-rises reflecting some broken man's
teeth. Circling birds marvel at that one old tree, across from Bangkok
Gardens, which has failed to resurrect this spring. A tigerish
police dog drives away a homeless boy from the steps of United
Illuminating Company. "The mind of New Haven breaks
the back of New Haven," a crazed woman spits at the Green's
fountain. "Yale doesn't pay taxes. Why should I?" Clouds
flock over long-steepled churches. The wind combs the heads
of handsome oaks. In the Gothic shadow of Yale,
residents mill about like laboratory rats. "The rich hate
the poor and the poor kill each other," says a bumper sticker.
Beautification bleached Fair Haven. Prostitutes have turned
Ferry Street into a runway as cops circle the block
like sharks. A hulking Catholic Church looks on calm
as a monk. The Hill is a flat hell, where children breathe
death, gunshots peppering the air like horns. East Rock
and West Rock jut out of the city like fresh wounds. Stand
on East Rock Park and look down at the diverse face of New Haven
in crumbling houses and garden mansions. Orange
Street smells like dogs and blossoms. Edgewood Park nurses
serenity in Duck Pond. The Science Park doesn't feed Newhallville
jobs. As dark blooms, Gateway Community College lights up
like a chandelier. New Haven dances on Crown
Street, in Lazy Lizard, G.O.A.T, Alchemy, Elevate,

Empire and BAR. "Once the blood is gone
this summer," the crazed woman barks,
pointing at staggering students, "New Haven will fall
into a coma." Avenues Whitney, Whalley and Dixwell snake
into the leaves of Hamden. The skunky Long Island Sound
remixes the highway's lullaby. Good streets lie
next to bad streets as the city closes its eyes.

ON THE NIGHT OBAMA WON
THE PRESIDENCY

Leaves fall in the lap of a cemetery,
the sky full of unpicked cotton. The Jamaican
clerk at the corner store, who would be there
until the sun woke up, rattles on. I try
to remain calm, speechless, let the victory
heal centuries of stings. I collect my Sunny
Delight and depart as a giant brown woman
raises a storm about a winning lotto ticket
that's a loser. Out in the wind, I can feel
a people rise. The night seems
warmer. A black man in a black
car yells, "Hell, yeah" to me as the stoplight
turns from red to green. I chuckle. On Putnam
a thick old black man, with a bull dog, raises
his fist to me across the street,
and for a few seconds we volley words
about a sea-changing night. By the pine-hidden
retirement home a forgetful white man asks me
for a dollar. I hand him a five and wish
him merry Christmas when he tries
to hand back change. The moon gazes
at itself in the reservoir as water crashes blindly
over the dam. Would this be the night
I felt less Jamaican, and more American?
In the arboreal hill between mansions a cop
draws his gun and wants to know
what I'm doing walking around at 12.
I tell him who I am and he says, "You walked
all the way from Southern Connecticut State
University?" I nod and march on with the peace
of King on Birmingham.

CHILDREN WITH WILLIAMS SYNDROME HAVE NO RACIAL BIASES

—Title of Yahoo article

You think the world is beautiful
until you read about kids battling
a syndrome that makes them
dead to racism. The N-word hasn't lost
 its teeth, I feel. Hearing black
and white kids in back of the bus
calling each other it in friendship
makes me a slave, makes me feel
welts over my back and a rope burning
my neck, makes me want to live
in that Louis Armstrong song
"What a Wonderful World." Forgetting
is progress I fear, as buzzards unfold
like umbrellas in the lightning wind. Tarps
flap like caged birds in the market distance.
The breaks scream. And kids storm out,
race towards Goodwill in the sunny rain.
The stoplight says green but the bus cannot
move, the avenue jammed as hulls.

FERRY STREET

The cathedral is a huge relief,
heaven in hell all red-brown bricks and calm,
with iron-looking wooden doors
and no fence. Across
the street in front of a white corner
shop candles and teddy
bears mark the murder of a boy around
a rain-darkened light pole. Alive,
little boys pull down a tire-based
basketball hoop to dunk an airless
basketball. It must be twenty
degrees out, but a prostitute in nothing
but a tight white silk dress confuses
traffic. You can smell the Atlantic
or the salty drains stuffed with crack
the police can't find. A drug-headed
girl dances when she walks. I look back
up at the rusty spire disappearing
in the sunny clouds. Candles burn
in every window of the rectory
and every business advertises in half
Spanish. Bullet-riddled pines shade
a lot. The three-story houses are falling
down but standing up. There are no
Obama signs and I am forced to beg
God for the indoor calm of the cathedral
as an old woman waves
to me from a baby stroller.

WEST HAVEN, CONNECTICUT

Gulls bask in the ungodly
breath of the Long Island Sound. The sun
ripens like the smile
of a black goddess storming
the beach. The Sound drums ceaselessly
against the shore as traffic thunders
on the avenues. It's January,
but the budding beeches think
it's March. Rotting houses
battle for space like the overcrowded
teeth of truant boys playing
basketball on a snow-covered court
as upbraiding seniors leak out of their condos
and flood the concrete boardwalk.
Beachside mansions struggle to outshine
each other like pageant
contestants in lurid evening
gowns. But the sky's still as empty
as a drunk's wallet as he wobbles
home. The penetrating
sound of a sick train arouses
hope in everyone.

CREEP

The first time a woman called him
a creep he was studying the storm
of her hair in a park touched by fall
and twilight. He loved the way the dying
leaves danced and died around her
beauty, one clinging to her shoulder
before plummeting
into this grave of a world.
She sat on a bench, opening her heart
and mind to impossibilities, he imagined.
The way he was sitting across
from her on another park bench, inhaling
her garden scents, rehearsing non-creepy
ways to explain to her that her freckles
reminded him of stars on a lonely
night in a lonely lake. How her red
lips reminded him of unpicked apples
in a lost summer. The lake
watched as he walked up
to her and asked what she thought
of the current political climate
and the great trees shook their great
heads as he looked into the universe
of her eyes and knew there would be
no heaven, after all.

DANCING WITH HURRICANE SANDY

Fred feels all Hurricane Sandy
wants is a willing dance partner
before she dies. That makes sense,
he thinks, sitting on his heavenly
couch, with a beer which he downs
like medicine. "What's the difference
between Sandy and a ducky high school
girl who couldn't go to the homecoming
dance because she couldn't get a date?"
he wants to ask his wife of five winters,
but he knows his wife hates Sandy
and she says as much when the light
goes out. She believes monsters
should stay away from civilized
folks, but when her phone chirps and she picks it
up, Fred can hear the bulldozing voice
of the construction worker who Fred
thinks has been entering her. Fred looks
through the window and sees Sandy
dancing with everything. Still on the phone,
going upstairs, his wife breaks
into laughter and doesn't seem
to care anymore about the dark.
Fred drinks another beer and prays
for a way to go outside and join
Sandy but the doors and windows
are boarded up and he can't remember
where his wife put the front door
key and he doesn't trust the keys of his reason,
but when he tries the door it miraculously
opens and he steps outside in the massaging
dark and takes Sandy's hand, knowing
he can never give it back.

AFTER A DIVORCE

A loony hot sun in a stampede
of clouds, desiccated wind-strummed
leaves, sleepless nights, days, therapeutic
social work classes, a dronelike punched
pond-size hole in the university's parking
lot, hell dates, breakups, break downs,
biting cold, elusive women embodying
happiness, death of summer hearsed
on the wind, winter waking up
against heaters, more earthquake
heartbreaks, avalanches of kids at work,
babies protesting, homeless laughing,
a "happy birthday" balloon stuck in a cemetery
tree, lovers fussing or kissing in a dark mirror
lake, a helicopter whining, the sea applauding,
what I would tell an Alien about the heart
of life here on earth. There is love;
and there is the absence of love
which infects everything.

ON HEARING THAT JERK FISH JAMAICAN RESTAURANT CLOSED FOR GOOD

[Hamden, CT]

There's a sadness at the heart
of everything. Trees rock like old women
at a funeral. The sun swims lonely
as a goldfish in a cloudy bowl. The yellow walls
are still yellow and green. The potted palm tree
doesn't wave to me. The novel-long menu,
in green on the wall over the register, reads
like an epitaph on a tombstone. You
couldn't get half the food on the menu,
like you could never find Jamaica
in America. The jerk fish wasn't jerked
but baked with deceit. The cashiers all had voices
like shady rivers. Like the sort of women I dreamt
of marrying, their every word dipped in tropical
sweetness, their smiles, heat in winter. The owner,
a saccharine dictator, whipped his staff with payless
insults, charming the green out of customers.
Now it's like a dead cow being gutted
for organs. Sandwiched between Subway
and Marshalls. Gone are the bright waves
of peaceful smells. The little country I could wander
into and breathe in reggae music like sea
breeze. The wicker chairs soft as sand.

ACROPOLIS ALL NIGHT DINER

The waitresses are sleep
fighting wakefulness. Snow
furs the avenue. All the men
fall for the pretty Greek hostess
whose yellow vampirish smile
shines like winter-clouded
streetlights, her lean body lithe
as lilies in spring wind, her eyes white
hot cloudless moonlight. Christmas
lights still hug the diner like a rapper's
gold chains. Red lights reflect red
eyes. A graying couple whisper
like bees in a far corner. A blonde
admonishes her elderly lover
for loving his wife more
than his goddess. A solitary black
man sips tea, his troubled eyes
swaying to oppressive snowflakes
as a truck rumbles by and we shake
until we feel we're on a ship
unable to leave shore.

HELEN OF NEW HAVEN

Wears punched-warped braces
and a rebellious weave frames
a face ripe with so much beauty
neighborhoods kill each other
to win her smile. Her uncles, she says,
shot an older family friend who forcibly
entered her when she was sixteen. She regrets
and doesn't regret that the family friend
had to die. But she bears the hell of knowing
her sweet uncles are buried
in prison. She has a voice like Bey and skin
the color of streetlights. Her voice is money.
She speaks and flies into song. Her mother
tried to kill her philandering father
in his sleep, by having him
inhale poison and by beating his head
with a washed pot. Helen believes
death and love are stalking her.
She doesn't like to be in the same room
with a man she doesn't love.
Mostly she wants to kill her psychic
pain. Her daughter is peace in a bullet-riddled
night. Helen wishes to erase
her abusive baby's father for standing her up
for a next bird. Her lover, not her baby's
father, beat two murder cases
and she still uses him
to release, no kissing,
because she knows
he's guilty.

MY ALCOHOLIC BARBER

Cuts like a lawn mover, rambling
about his fourteen children by four women
who will always never love him the way
life will never love him. His cell blares
Tupac's "Thugs get lonely too." He confesses
he needs to hurry up before the liquor
store shuts up. He used to be
a hood doctor dispensing medication
to damaged souls, now his voice washes
the dealers from his street. Though tagged
a felon, he fell into an overnight job
at a grocery store which hates him. His kids
eat all his paychecks. He worships hard
cash. No tip because I risked my life to be cut
on his blind porch in a gun-happy
neighborhood. Cop cars flash and frighten.
Razor bumps fear him.
He held his first gun at four to meet black
power. He claims to be barber
deity when I point out my zigzagging
beard, the patches in my hair.
While he fixes me, he says he's been in over
a hundred women and knows what to do
about my inability to enter women who come
back to my midnight apartment. "Turn off
the lights and take off your clothes," he says.
"That's the trick. To act like it happened
before it does." He sweeps the shear
over my hair, covering
mistakes with mistakes.

HE REGRETS

He regrets never being
handsome enough to enter
a goddess named April
when he was green.
He regrets looking out
the hospital window at the idle
sun gentrifying
ancient swaying trees.
He regrets dying, his last days
falling away like so many leaves.

STATUS

I'm lost and don't need to be
found in love, my cell, regrets
and rejections, praying for a sky-clearing
text/email, WhatsApp/Oovoo/Facebook
message, witty status, call….The people
I hate I used to love violently, dear Mother,
Father, Sis, Bro. I love for lightning
to lash a somber day, the sun to die
with my longing. Looking at the big picture.
I'm here but I could be there in an orgy
or safely in a jeep while lions frolic.
I'm tired of thinking in loud. I'm happy,
long-headed, bucktoothed,
too many teeth like a piano, pensive,
passive, tall, a speech impediment,
30, Jamaican-American.
Who isn't tired of love and loss? We want
to sleep and live in a movie and direct
our lives like God and make the world
over in our sad happiness. My laptop's
antivirus goes on about "restoring...the icon
in the system" and I think about the black
goddess I'm obsessed with who claims
to only love white men, because, among
other delusions, they are less shady. The famous
comedian I'll never become because I am
stuck taming anger. I shave days off
my days in a greasy buffet. But people's voices
grate at my loneliness. One basketball player
trash-talks another basketball player is the top
headline on ESPN.com. When did we become
so lost in trash, all this nothing claiming

to be gold? I wear my desperation
like a clown. Kids cry. My phone whines, dies.
I don't know if the birds are crying or singing
or both, dear heaven.

SECOND DAY OF NEW JOB AS AN
INNER-CITY EMPLOYMENT SPECIALIST

Early again with no
one home at work
to annihilate
my pride. I don't
yet have a key
to my future
as my past.
The office waits
for me like a bucking
horse, like a warm sea
too deep.

OUT IN THE NEW CENTURY

Out in the new century,
everybody lost in cell
phones, clouds aspiring
to be rain, rain needling
the fabric of bushlands.
City-reflected eyes say tired,
even the dogs whining away
twilight. We have dreams
that take us to riches
and back to paycheck
to paycheck, squawking
kids. We worry a mistake will
cost us work and how
will hope survive on no
cash? On the news, America
wrestles the world as Ebola erases
humanity. No one's in love
with reality. The preacher says
love is on its way but lost. Night,
stampeding college
students light up the city and drink
until they become babes
unable to think, talk and walk.
A sunny dentist can't find
your pain. Chiming music
from an ice cream truck reminds
us life is not a horror movie.

WHALLEY AVENUE, NEW HAVEN

It bleeds out of New Haven and smells
like the smoky chicken the Jamaican
Rasta jerks on the sidewalk grille to seduce
stomachs. Don't mind the boarded-up
vision center. The pregnant
prostitutes. "You lonely?" One lady will
say when you ask for directions.
Say yes, but no. A woman
sits on a toppled shopping cart
like a statue after an interminable day
of work at a Stop and Shop that pays
only enough to catch the turtling
bus. Cops comb the dark begging
for trouble. The drug lords
have survived the war against
winter and flash diamond smiles
at every car. The Yale students hurry
from the heart of the organic stores.
The Indian clerks in Sam's sing in
another language to beat off sleep.
When the hungry post clubbing revelers
pour into the store and begin to bemoan
the lack of soul foods and police
brutality, the clerk does not argue
with 400 years of anger.

2 AM, NEW HAVEN

In spring all night neighbors
argue on pollinic porches as babies
cry like background singers. "Come
in the house," the man begs
and traffic drowns her answer.
The war against allergies cannot
be fought. My roommate
is as big as his room and speaks
like a man searching for himself.
Everything he says blooms
into existential questions. "Why
are there empty cups in the fridge?"
he says, but means why are our lives
so empty even as we fill our days
finding love on Okcupid. The Bulls
and the Cavaliers battle to playoff
death on TV. The players
resemble a Greek war. Everybody's
limping on the court and looking
for the ref to blow the whistle on time.
I retreat to my blind, four-windowed
room, tune my computer to a woman
opening her world so I can jerk
off loneliness.

RED NIGHT

[Orchard Street, New Haven, CT]

Red lights like a three-eyed monster
over traffic in the sooty dark, red everywhere
in memorials around keeling light
poles, desert wine bottles, flowers dried up
like love, teddy bears lounging like deadbeat
fathers watching TV as life huffs by, sneakers
hanging from live wires like men in Jim Crow. Red
cries. Who I am but black
and alive tonight? My Sentra is not quiet,
not quite blood red. Poverty shot
another brother. The news says
the victim was the suspect. I mean a black
man shot a black man shot a black man, probably
over coke, the drug not the drink. And you think
of death and look at the sky which is all
smiles because the moon is naked again
tonight, no clouds, no clothes, no way
to hide that we are hurting so we extinguish
ourselves and each other. These houses
live across from a cemetery, from death,
heaven or hell. And you think happiness,
so vague—what does it really mean
to part the Red Sea of oppression?
To drive and wear red, feeding on pain
and power as boys basketball in old snow by
sputtering streetlights. I bump up the music
to cheer up the hood. Kids shake as my car
crawls around a liquor store. The lyrics, poison,
the beat, the cure. Business is booming
for funeral homes too. Men swagger
with brown paper bags or yell

as they whisper to a strutting
black woman so beautiful you want to be
more than you are. She's decked for the club
all heels. And legs and a red dress so tight it boils
your blood and overheats your senses.
You want to stop but you do not stop.
Her natural hair like something out
of your garden.

Special Thanks

I want to thank a number of people for their continued support. I want to thank my mother, Marcia Chambers; my father, Lenford Lennon; my brother and sister, Sheldon and Dezeta. My friends, colleagues and co-workers: Ariana Shapiro, Tim Parrish, Steve Larocco, Jeff Mock, Vivian Shipley, Dana Sonnenschein, Catherine Di Leo, Robin Troy, Tyreece Gary (artist of cover artwork), Ashley Greene, Nakisha Jones, Jose Dejesus, Mary Reynolds, Honella Davis, Ingrid Derek-Lewis, Shanna Walker Johnson, Public Allies, Mark Cameron, Melissa Mason, Florestine Taylor, Apreia Cooper, Clinton Cain, Ebony Murphy-Root, Olivia Whittle, Meghan Trupp, Lynnette Johnson, Brandon Hutchinson, Baub Bidon, Frederick-Douglass Knowles II, Maria Fisher, Sean Igoe, Lori DeSanti (for helping me edit the book), Amy Ashton, Oye Imoisili, Ms. Bea and Ms. Bradley; New Haven and Jamaica. New Light High School, Larry Conaway, Lisa Loeb, Samantha Lynn, Leanora Harper, Rufina Harper, Vivienne Harper, Ernel Grant, Mrs. Brown, Mr. and Mrs. Stuart, Sherman Malone, Savitra Jones, Dana Krofssik, Samantha Dagesse, Cassidy O'Brien, Val Mckee, Nikki Farrow, Heather Swanson, Alicia Wright, Cavel Wright, Heather Wright, James Hill Primary School, Trout Hall All Age School, Clarendon College, Sonia Jackson, Benjamin Kowalsky, Sharon Anderson, Sister Anderson, the Southern Connecticut State University English and Social Work departments, God, and M. Scott Douglass.